The Old Hospital

I Talk You Talk Press

CONTENTS

CHAPTER ONE

Steven, James and Imran are university students in Manchester. They share a student apartment. The apartment is a few miles from the university. Steven is from Manchester. James is from Glasgow, and Imran is from Birmingham. Now, they are sitting in Steven's bedroom. They are eating noodles and drinking beer. It is October 30th. One day before Halloween.

Steven and Imran are first year students. They are new. They arrived in September. James is a third year student. He has lived in the apartment for two years. Steven and Imran are asking James questions about life at the university. James is telling them many things.

"Do you know the story of these apartments?" asks James.

"No," says Imran. "What story?"

"Well, the building next to these apartments is an old hospital," says James.

"Yes, I know," says Imran. "It looks scary at night. How old is it?"

"It is a hundred and fifty years old. But it closed about thirty years ago," says James. "Before it closed, this area had many hospital buildings. These apartments were part of the old hospital. There were many people in the hospital. Many doctors, nurses and patients. The hospital has a sad history."

"A sad history? Why?" asks Imran.

"Well, it has a ghost story," says James. "All the students here know the story."

"A ghost story?" asks Steven. "Tell us!"

"Well, doctors usually help people. They care for their patients. But there was one doctor called Dr Rigby. He was not a nice doctor. About fifty years ago, strange things happened at the hospital. Patients were dying."

"But many patients die in hospital. That is not strange," says Imran.

"But the patients did not have big problems. They were not very ill. But after Dr Rigby saw them, they died. At first, the other doctors and nurses did not think it was strange. But when the fifth patient died after seeing Dr Rigby, they thought something was strange.

"They called the police. The police asked Dr Rigby many questions. I don't know the details, but they found the answer. Dr Rigby gave the patients too much medicine and they died."

"Why did he give them too much medicine?" asks Steven.

"Because he wanted to kill them. He was a very bad doctor. He didn't want to help people. He wanted to kill them! After that, he went to prison."

"That's a terrible story," says Imran. "So who is the ghost? Is it one of the patients?"

"The ghost is Dr Rigby," says James. "He killed himself with a knife in prison. A few years ago, some students went into the hospital at night. They heard many strange noises. Then, they saw a man. The man came out of an office. He was wearing a white coat. But the coat was not all white. It was also red. Blood red. The man was a ghost. The ghost was looking at them and he was laughing. He said to the students, 'You will die!'

"The students were very scared. They screamed and ran away. The next day, one of the students was driving his car in the centre of Manchester. A bus hit his car, and he died. It was very strange. Everyone said, 'The ghost of Dr Rigby killed him.'"

"That's scary," says Imran. "I don't like it."

"Now, no students go into the old hospital. They think if they go into the hospital, they will see the ghost of Dr Rigby. And maybe, something bad will happen. Maybe they will die."

Steven laughs. "I don't believe it," he says. "The students wanted to make a scary story. And the car accident, well, I think it was just an accident. The student was unlucky. Manchester roads are very busy. He was a young driver. He didn't have much driving experience."

"It's true!" says James. "Ask the other students! They will tell you the same story!"

Steven drinks some more beer. "Let's go into the hospital. Tomorrow night is Halloween. Let's go then!"

"I'm not going!" says Imran.

"And I'm not going!" says James.

"OK, I will go alone," says Steven.

Imran and James look at Steven. "You say you will go, but I don't think you will go," says James.

"OK," says Steven. "I will find something in the hospital and bring it back here."

"What will you bring?" asks Imran.

"I don't know. But maybe there are old files, or something. I will bring something. I'm not scared of Dr Rigby! I don't believe in ghosts! Nothing bad will happen to me!"

CHAPTER TWO

The next day, James tells many students about Steven's plan. The students are excited.

"Really? Is he really going to go into the hospital?" they ask. "That's cool!"

But some students are worried. "If he goes into the hospital, something bad may happen. Maybe he will die! And it is Halloween," they say.

In the afternoon, Steven goes to look at the hospital. It is a cloudy day, and the old hospital looks dark and scary. It is an old stone building. There is a big clock tower. There are many windows. There is a gate, and a high wall all around the hospital.

Maybe I shouldn't go into the hospital, he thinks. *Maybe James' story is true. But it is too late now. All the students know about my plan. If I say 'I'm not going to go into the hospital', they will laugh at me. They will think I am weak. I have to go. But it looks scary.*

Then, Steven laughs. *It is only a story. There is no ghost! There is no Dr Rigby! I will be OK! And all the other students will think I am cool! But how can I get into the hospital tonight? The gate and wall are very high.*

He walks around. There are no holes in the wall.

Maybe I can climb over it, he thinks. *But I must be careful.*

CHAPTER THREE

In the evening, the students put on their Halloween costumes. James is wearing a ghost costume. Imran is wearing a monster costume. They come into Steven's bedroom.

"What do you think about our costumes?" asks Imran.

"You look great!" says Steven.

James looks worried. "Steven, I think you should come to the party. Don't go to the hospital. Something bad might happen. You will enjoy the party. It is your first Halloween party at university. All the students are going. Will you come with us?"

Steven says, "No. I am going into the hospital. I went there this afternoon. Now, I am interested in it. I want to go inside. It looks exciting! Have a good time at the party. I will see you when you come home."

"OK," says James. "But be careful. If you have any problems, call me or send me a message."

"I will be OK! Stop worrying!" says Steven.

James and Imran go out of the apartment. Steven is alone. He looks out of the window. It is very quiet. All the other students are at the Halloween party. Steven looks at the sky. There is a full moon.

At 10:00pm, Steven leaves the apartment and locks the door. He walks out of the apartment building. It is cold outside. The Halloween party is in the centre of the city, so there are no students in the apartments. All the apartment windows are dark. He walks quickly to the hospital. He stands and looks at it. The moon is shining bright in the sky. The hospital looks very scary at night. There are many trees around the gate, and there are many shadows. He can hear the wind, blowing through the trees.

I don't want to do this, he thinks. *But I have to do it.*

He climbs over the high gate. He uses the light on his smartphone to look around.

He hears a noise.

What's that? he thinks. The noise is in the trees. He looks up at the trees with his smartphone light and sees a bird.

It's a bird. It's only a bird. Relax, Steven!

He walks towards the hospital.

How can I get into the hospital? he thinks. *I hope the door is unlocked.*

He walks to the large front door and tries to open it. It is locked.

I will try the back door, he thinks. He walks around to the back. The hospital is big, so it takes a few minutes. He tries to open the back door, but it is locked.

What can I do? Maybe I should go back to the apartment. I can say 'The door was locked, so I couldn't go in'. But no, I must go in. If I don't, everyone will laugh at me. Maybe there is a broken window.

He walks around the building again. He looks at the windows.

Here! he thinks. *Here is a broken window!*

The broken window is big. He can climb through it. He looks around.

OK, I'm going in! he thinks. He climbs in through the window and enters the hospital.

CHAPTER FOUR

Inside the hospital it is very dark. Steven uses the light from his smartphone to look around. He is in a very big room. There are many old beds. There are old curtains on some of the windows.

The beds are still here! he thinks. He walks through the room, looking at the beds. They are very old, and made of metal.

Maybe they are fifty years old, he thinks. *Maybe, Dr Rigby killed people in these beds. I don't like this. I want to go back to the apartment.*

He walks out of the room. He is in a long hall. There are many doors at the sides of the hall. He stops and listens carefully. It is very quiet.

I can't hear anything, he thinks. *There is no ghost in here!*

He opens one of the doors. It is an old office. There is a desk, and a chair.

I can't take a desk or a chair, he thinks. *They are too big and heavy. I need to take something small.*

He looks in the next room, but the room is empty. Then, he sees a sign on a door. The sign says, 'Doctor's Room'.

He opens the door and goes in. He looks around. It is a big room. There are many desks and chairs. There are no files on the desks.

What can I take? There is nothing to take! thinks Steven. *If I can't find anything to take, I can take a photograph. If I have a photograph, the students will believe me. I can put it on Facebook! Everyone will like it!*

Then, he sees something hanging on the back of the door.

What's that? A white coat! he thinks. *A doctor's coat! I can take that! If I take the coat, James and Imran and all the other students will believe me!*

He takes the white coat from the hanger on the back of the door. He goes out of the room and closes the door. He listens carefully again. He cannot hear anything inside the hospital. He can only hear the wind outside.

There is no ghost here! he thinks.

"Dr Rigby, where are you? Come on Dr Rigby, show me your face!" he says.

He waits, but no ghost comes. He laughs.

There is no ghost here, he thinks again.

He opens Facebook and sends a message to Imran and James.

---How is your party? Are you having a good time? I am in the hospital now! I have something! I will show you it tonight! Come to my room after the party! ---

He goes back to the window and climbs out of the hospital. It is cold outside, so he puts the coat on.

This coat is my size! he thinks. *I look like a doctor! This is cool!*

"Nice to NOT meet you Dr Rigby!" he shouts. He laughs and runs to the gate. He climbs over the gate and runs back to his apartment wearing the white coat.

CHAPTER FIVE

Steven is sitting in his bedroom. He is waiting for James and Imran to return. He puts the white coat on a hanger on the back of his bedroom door.

They will be very surprised to see this, thinks Steven. *They will tell everyone. All the students will think I am very strong!*

At around 1:00am, James and Imran return. They look tired.

"So, did you go into the hospital?" asks Imran.

"I don't think he did," says James. "I think he was too scared. I think he stayed in the apartment and watched TV!"

Steven laughs. "I didn't stay in the apartment! I went to the hospital!"

"Did you bring anything to show us?" asks James.

Steven walks to the door and takes the white coat off the hanger. He gives it to James.

"Look at this," he says. "I found this white coat in the doctor's office."

James touches the coat. "Wow, you really did it!" he says. "You really went to the hospital!"

"Of course," says Steven.

"Was it scary?" asks Imran.

"No, not at all," says Steven. He doesn't tell his friends he was scared.

"Maybe this is Dr Rigby's coat!" says Imran.

James throws the coat at Steven. "You got Dr Rigby's coat! His ghost will come tonight!"

Steven laughs. "I don't believe in ghosts. There is no ghost of Dr Rigby! It's just a doctor's coat. That's all!"

Imran looks at the coat. "It looks old," he says. "Maybe fifty years old. I don't like it."

James goes to the kitchen to get a glass of water.

"How was the party?" asks Steven.

"It was good," says Imran. "All the students were there. Everyone wore interesting costumes. Some people asked me, 'Where is Steven?' I said, 'He is going into the hospital.' Everyone said, 'Wow, that's cool! He is so strong!' Everyone was very surprised. They want to talk to you about it tomorrow."

Steven feels proud. *Everyone wants to talk to me. I will become popular,* he thinks. *Maybe some girls will want to date me!*

James comes back from the kitchen.

"I drank too much tonight," he says. "I'm going to go to bed."

"Me too," says Imran. "I am very tired. Good night Steven. Don't have bad dreams!"

Steven laughs. "I'm OK," he says. He puts the coat on the hanger and closes the door behind James and Imran. He gets into bed and switches the light off. He goes to sleep.

CHAPTER SIX

Bang! Bang! Bang!

Steven jumps up. *What is that?* he thinks. *Someone is knocking on my door!*

He looks at the clock. It is 4:00am.

"James? Imran? What are you doing? It's four am!" he shouts.

"Open the door! This is the police!" says a voice.

"The police?" says Steven. "What?"

"Open the door!" says the voice again.

Steven gets out of bed and opens the door. There are two policemen. Behind them are James and Imran. They look scared.

"What is it? What's happened?" asks Steven.

"Are you Steven Walker?" asks the policeman.

"Yes, why?" asks Steven.

"We need to talk to you. Please come to the living room," says the policeman.

Steven, James and Imran go into the living room with the policemen. Steven sits on the floor. One of the policemen sits on the sofa. The other policeman says, "May I check your bedroom?"

"Sure," says Steven. The other policeman goes out of the living room.

"What is it?" Steven asks the other policeman.

"Mr Walker, we have some bad news. This morning, at around three am, a woman heard screams from your family's house. She lives in the next house. She went outside, and she saw a man, wearing a white coat. The man was running out of your family's house. The white coat was covered in blood. The woman ran into the house, and she found your mother and father and sister. I'm sorry, to tell you this, but…they are dead."

"What?!" shouts Steven.

"Someone killed them with a knife. We think it is the man wearing the white coat."

Steven starts to cry. James says, "I can't believe this."

"I know this is very difficult for you. But we must ask you some questions. We must find the man. It was dark, so the woman did not see his face. She just saw the white coat. And the blood."

Then, the other policeman comes into the living room. He looks very serious.

"What is this?" he asks.

He is holding the white coat from the hospital. But now, the coat is not white. The coat is red. It is covered in blood. The blood is fresh.

"What? I…I…I can't believe it!" says Steven.

The policemen look at Steven. "Where were you at three am this morning?" asks one of the policemen.

"I was asleep, in my bed," says Steven.

"So what is this? Why do you have a white coat? Why is the white coat covered in blood?"

"I…I…I went into the old hospital. There is a ghost story about the hospital. About a man called Dr Rigby. I don't believe in ghosts. I wanted to go into the hospital because it was Halloween. I found the white coat in an office. I brought it back here to show my friends. Then, I hung it on the back of my door, and I went to sleep."

The policemen walk over to Steven. They hold his arms tightly.

"You are coming to the police station with us!" says one of the policemen. "We want to ask you questions about this!"

They take Steven out of the living room.

"James, Imran! Help me!" says Steven. "I didn't do anything! I didn't kill my family!"

"Be quiet!" says a policeman. They walk out of the apartment and close the door.

James and Imran look at each other. They cannot believe it.

"Do you think Steven killed his family?" asks Imran.

"No, I don't," says James quietly. "He was in bed. It's Dr Rigby," says James quietly. "It's Dr Rigby…"

THANK YOU

Thank you for reading The Old Hospital! We hope you enjoyed the story. (Word count: 3,023)

There are quizzes about this book on our free study site I Talk You Talk Press EXTRA. http://italk-youtalk.com

If you would like to read more graded readers, please visit our website
http://www.italkyoutalk.com

Other Level 1 graded readers include
A Business Trip to New York
A Homestay in Auckland
A Trip to London
Dear Ellen
Haruna's Story Part 1
Haruna's Story Part 2
Haruna's Story Part 3
Ken's Story Part 1
Ken's Story Part 2
Life is Surprising!
Strange Stories
The Christmas Present
We Met Online

ABOUT THE AUTHOR

I Talk You Talk Press is a Japan-based publisher of language textbooks, graded readers and language learning/teaching resources.

Our team is made up of highly experienced language teachers and translators, who have all studied at least one additional language to an advanced level.

This experience enables us to design our materials from the perspective of both the teacher and the learner. We consult with both teachers and language learners when designing our textbooks and graded readers, and test our materials extensively in the classroom before publication.

We are a fast-growing press, and currently publish graded readers for learners of English. We publish new graded readers monthly.

The Old Hospital

The Old Hospital

The Old Hospital

www.ingramcontent.com/pod-product-compliance
Lightning Source LLC
Chambersburg PA
CBHW022353040426
42449CB00006B/854